WITTY ST

WITTY STORIES
OF
THE HODJA

Retold by
Vimala Arangaden

Rupa & Co

Contents

Stories of the Hodja

The Turkish people tell a story. A school master of their's, they say, more than five hundred years ago, was one day dealing with some of his naughty boys for the pranks they had played. He called the boys one at a time, asked what part each had played in the mischief, and sternly pronounced the punishment.

And so he came to the last one. It was Nasiruddin who was always present where anything happened. The master looked solemnly at the boy, over his thick moustache and bushy beard. "And what did you do?" he asked slowly but firmly.

Nasiruddin's capped head hung low, his chin almost touching his chest, and his feet together at attention.

"Speak!" the master ordered.

"Effendi... Sir!" the boy stammered. "I ... I... did nothing! I... only watched and laughed."

"Laughed?" The master thought for a minute for the right punishment for one who just watched and laughed.

"As long as the world lasts," he pronounced, "people will laugh at you."

So for all these hundreds of years, the people of Turkey, young and old, have laughed at the doings of Nasiruddin. Not only they but the people in the countries around them, and now, with the telling of these stories in more languages of the world, people all over the world still laugh at the name of Nasiruddin Hodja, who grew up to be a teacher and priest, and acquired the title of Hodja which followed his name.

Nasiruddin's faithful companion and friend was his patient longeared donkey—the inseparable partner of any Turkish villager.

Hundreds of stories have been told of the Hodja, and some, they say are true. But it is a fact that in the reign of Tamerlane the Great, the Mongol conqueror, there was a teacher-priest whose name was Nasiruddin Hodja, who lived in the town of Ak Shehir in Turkey, and who was well-known for being both wise and foolish at the same time.

Even at his grave people laugh, for it is not like any other grave. The grave stands at the top of a hill near Ak Shehir. It is known by a single iron gate which stands there carefully locked, but without any walls around.

The Hodja is to Turkey what Tenali Raman is to South India and Birbal to North India.

The Hodja Shoots Arrows

Tamerlane always enjoyed the company of the simple Hodja. He was unlike his courtiers who kept praising him just to gain his favour. To the Hodja, every man was the same, and he spoke sincerely from his heart.

On a lovely spring morning Tamerlane and the Hodja set out to watch the soldiers practising archery. Actually the Hodja had planned to plant onions in his garden that day. But he needed no better excuse to put off this backbreaking work.

It was one of those fine mornings which infuses new life and strength into one. The old Hodja became a new man — a younger and stronger man. As he walked with the Emperor, he even grew very brave — able to do just anything — possible and impossible.

They were soon where the soldiers were practising. A soldier shot straight into the bull's eye of the target. "Good shot!" yelled the Hodja. To the Emperor he whispered, "This reminds me of the days when I was young and used a bow and arrow."

"You! An archer!" exclaimed the Emperor in great surprise. "I never heard that before!"

"Oh yes," the Hodja went on, "I was an expert archer. Men would come from far to see me shoot. How I would love to get a bow and arrow in my hands again!"

"Bring me a bow and arrow," the Emperor ordered. To the Hodja he said: "You show my men some real archery." And Tamerlane held out the bow and arrow to him.

This the Hodja did not expect. He was speechless. But his mind worked very fast.

"It is not fair, your Majesty," he said, "to waste your soldiers' precious time."

"Watching a good shot is valuable learning," the Emperor answered. The Hodja was feeling very uncomfortable now. "It's a long time, Your Majesty," he said, "since I held a bow and arrow in my hand." "A skilled archer never forgets his skill, Nasiruddin," the Emperor persisted.

"How to get out of this trap?" The Hodja thought hard.

He set the arrow in place and aimed it. Just then he saw a soldier aiming at the target.

"Wait," the Hodja gestured to him.

The Hodja walked up to the soldier and took the bow and the aimed arrow and shot.

The arrow zoomed to almost the bull's eye. Then he went back to the king and said "Can't you see? I haven't touched a bow in ages!"

"And then — there is this cut…" he added, looking painfully at a slight scratch on his finger.

"You don' t have to touch either the bow or the arrow with

that finger," Tamerlane insisted, and a new bow and arrow was thrust into Nasiruddin's hands.

"The pain is in my shoulder, Your Majesty," Nasiruddin continued. "Did you not tell me this morning," asked the Emperor, "that the warm sunshine has burned your pain away?"

The Hodja could think of no more excuses. He saw that Tamerlane was bent on seeing the Hodja shoot. He could not possibly disobey or escape.

"Why yes, I did say that..." The Hodja tried to put on a bold look as he lifted the bow with his clumsy hands, and strode off with the arrow. A quick look at the practising soldiers showed him which way to hold the two. After trying a little, even the arrow almost fitted right. Screwing his eyes to look at the target, he pulled the bowstring.

The arrow fell a few inches from his feet.

Tamerlane watched the Hodja. He must surely get angry or at least feel ashamed! But not Hodja Nasiruddin. The old cocky grain spread across his face.

"That,"said he, "is to show how your Chief Huntsman shoots!"

Then the Hodja took another arrow and fitted it to the bow, beaming cheerfully at the soldiers crowding around him. Then grandly he pulled on the string. The arrow shot up into the air. A dozen soldiers jumped aside to escape the falling arrow.

"And that," the Hodja said, even more cheerfully, "is how your Governor shoots."

A third arrow went off way to the right.

"That," said the Hodja with a broad smile, "is how the General shoots." Nasiruddin Hodja then took a fourth arrow. By now he was no more afraid. He fitted the arrow, tugged at the string, and let the arrow go where it wished.

This time, the arrow shot out as if it knew just where it had to go. It whizzed in between the laughing soldiers, went straight and fixed itself right in the centre of the bull's eye!

With open mouth and popping eyes the Hodja stared at the arrow trembling in the bull's eye!

"*Mash Allah!*" he said under his breath. "*Mash Allah!*" Then he was himself again.

"And that," he said, as indifferently as he could, "is how Nasiruddin Hodja shoots."

The Heat of a Candle

It was cold outside, and snow was falling. Inside the coffee house where the men of Ak Shehir were gathered, it was warm. And as they cupped their hands round their coffee mugs, and sipped the strong black coffee, their faces glowed with happiness. The warmer their bodies grew the more yarns they told, and the boasts grew louder and bigger. But perhaps no one could boast more than the Hodja. "Cold outside! I can stand outside all night in the open without a fire to warm me," the Hodja bragged. With that he hastily and noisily gulped large mouthfuls of another cup of the hot black stuff.

One man looked through the window at the falling snow. He shivered and said: "No one can do that!"

"Of course, I can do it," the Hodja insisted. "I'll do it this very night!" And he warmed his hands over the pan of burning coals in the centre of the room.

"You cannot!" exclaimed one.

"I will! And if there is but a spark around me to warm

me, I'll lose my bet, and I'll...I'll give you all a feast at my house if I lose."

The bet was taken.

That night while all his friends curled up in their warm beds Nasiruddin Hodja stood alone in the market square. The night was pitch-dark and the snow seemed heavier than usual. Nasiruddin Hodja stamped his feet and hugged himself, to keep in the little warmth that was in his small body. If he was not quick enough, the snow dropped down his neck and melted down his back. This seemed the longest of all nights.

Oh how sleepy he was getting! He could hardly keep his eyes open. But one must never go to sleep in the snow. He now jumped up and down to keep awake, and to keep his feet from freezing. He slapped his cold arms to make them feel; he pinched his nose to make sure it was still there.

Then he noticed the glow of a flickering candle. That was in Mohammad Ali's house on the other side of the square. He fixed his eyes on that glow. How bright it seemed in this darkness! It even seemed to make him feel warm just looking at it! The Hodja did not take his eyes off it. The glow also helped to keep his tired eyes open.

At last streaks of dawn began to melt the inky darkness. Soon the rooftops appeared and then the houses. Morning at last! Nasiruddin shivered his way home, dragging his heavy feet.

The Hodja's curious friends met him as he walked home. "How did you do it?" they asked, greatly admiring him.

"Did you really have nothing to warm you?"

"Nothing," said the Hodja.

"Nothing at all?"

"Nothing except the glow of a flickering candle in Mohammad Ali's house across the square." The Hodja saw no harm in looking at a candle, or telling about it.

"A candle!"

"Did you say a candle?" "Was it burning?" asked another.

"But," said the Hodja, "it was in Mohammad Ali's house on the other side of the square."

"Oh, but a lighted candle is a flame. And a flame gives heat. You were warming yourself by the heat of the candle. So you have lost your bet," said one.

"Yes," they all laughed, "you have lost your bet."

At first, the Hodja laughed too, thinking they were joking; but they were very serious. The Hodja for once was too tired to argue. He set off homewards.

"When shall we come to your house for the feast?" they called after him.

"Come at sunset," the Hodja called back.

The Hodja began to think hard.

That evening, some time after the Mullah had called the faithful to prayer, the Hodja's guests arrived.

"Please sit down," came the voice of the Hodja from the kitchen. "I hope you are not too hungry; the food is not ready yet. But it is cooking."

"Oh, we will wait; don't worry," called the men cheerfully. They waited. And they waited. Minutes became hours, but no sounds of dishes were heard. And there was no smell of food cooking, either. The guests were very hungry, and became curious.

"Just a little longer...it will be done soon," called the Hodja from inside.

"Can we come inside and help?" they asked.

"Sure, sure," said the Hodja. "Come in, come in."

The men rose and stretched their stiff legs, and slowly made their way to the kitchen.

As each man entered, there passed over his face a look of surprise, and a foolish grin. There stood the Hodja, on tiptoes, vigorously stirring the contents of a big copper vessel hanging from the ceiling. Way down below burned a little candle!

"Dont worry. This will soon boil and our meal will be ready," promised the Hodja. "I have a candle burning."

Pumpkins on Trees

It was one of those days when the Hodja thought of going to his vegetable patch to work. He sat astride his skinny donkey, his feet almost touching the ground on both sides, and slowly made his way there. He would have loved an excuse to keep him from working on his pumpkin patch, but he had no such luck today.

Nasiruddin decided that he would do a good day's work today. First he cleared the patch of dead leaves and stones, and weeded it. He then dug all round the roots, and broke up the hard earth, making it soft.

"Now the sun and air and water can come right down to your roots," he said lovingly to his plants. There were many lovely yellow pumpkins on the vines, and it made his heart glad to see them. "I think one or two are nearly ready for me to take back to Fatima," he thought to himself.

Fatima… the name made him think of his supper. She had promised to make stew with goat's milk today. His mouth was watering already. And the thought of supper made him hungry for lunch. "I have worked enough for this morning; maybe I'll eat my lunch."

Nasiruddin unwrapped the packed lunch his good wife Fatima had given him. "Fatima is a good cook," he said to himself, "and makes tasty pickles. I must thank Allah for her."

Lunch over, the Hodja realised it was very hot. "Let me rest a while," he said.

He had chosen a shady spot under a large walnut tree. But the sun was hot, and he was perspiring in the heat. He looked this way and that. "No one to laugh at my bald head" he said. He pulled off his turban, and wiped his perspiring wet head and face with it.

The heat made his head itch. He gave it a good scratch. And then... he thought of something.

"Fancy," he said to himself, "there is this great big walnut tree, with its spreading branches; and all it produces is tiny fruits — these walnuts. And, on the ground this weak pumpkin creeper grows great big fruits — the pumpkin. Now, if I had planned this, I would have made big trees grow large fruits, and delicate creepers small fruits. The huge walnut tree would grow large fruit like the pumpkin, and the thin pumpkin vine would produce little walnuts. There is not much sense in this, it seems to me."

While the Hodja was meditating on this a breeze had sprung up. The branches shook and the leaves trembled. Then a thin twig snapped somewhere, and with a slight crash, something came rushing down... plop! on the Hodja's bald head. It was a walnut — small but hard. The Hodja saw stars. He felt his head; and a round lump, the size of a walnut, soon began to form there.

"Allah, I am sorry," he said. "I am sorry for thinking myself wiser than you. You have taught me a good lesson. If the walnut tree had produced huge fruits like the pumpkin, and one of those had fallen on my bald head, what would have happened to me? I know now why you made the large tree bear small fruit; and the lowly vine, the large pumpkin, close to the ground. You are All-Wise, O Allah. All praise be to you."

God Willing

It was bed-time in the Hodja home. Fatima, his wife, was making the beds. The Hodja was at the window, carefully studying the night sky. "What will the weather be like tomorrow?" he wondered loudly.

"Whatever the weather," Fatima commented, "we will have enough to do. If it is wet, I will weave, *insha' Allah**; if it is sunny, I will go down to the river and wash clothes, *insha' Allah*."

"Well," announced the Hodja, " if the sun shines, I will plough tomorrow."

"*Insha' Allah,*" Fatima added.

"And, if it rains," the Hodja continued, deaf to his wife's correction, "I will go up to the hills and chop wood."

"Why can you not say *insha' Allah*?" Fatima pleaded. "You know we can do things only if God wills it."

---

* Insha' Allah — Allah (or God) willing

"If it rains, I chop; if it shines, I plough," the Hodja muttered, as he rolled on to his mattress.

All night Fatima had bad dreams of ill luck coming to her husband because he would not ask for God's protection. But the Hodja slept soundly, snoring loudly.

The next day, it was raining steadily: so Fatima went to her loom. Nasiruddin picked up his axe.

In the stable, the Hodja found that the rainy night had lamed the donkey. The poor animal certainly would not climb up to the hills; much less carry a load of wood. A good excuse to keep from work! But the whir of Fatima's loom reminded him. She would surely say that the donkey's lameness was Allah's punishment for not saying *insha' Allah*.

The Hodja unwillingly set off to go up to the hills, to chop wood and to carry it back himself. He had to pick his way along the uneven slushy pathway. As he walked along slowly, he suddenly heard voices. It came from the crossroads ahead. Always eager for a chat, he hastened his footsteps. Too late he discovered they were soldiers.

"Here you!" One of them took the Hodja by the shoulder. "Show the way to Karabash" he ordered.

"Kaa ..ra ..bash?" The Hodja pretended he had never heard the name before. Karabash! And he thought of the long trek up and down the hills — an awful journey even in the best weather. "Kaa ..ra ..bash," he shook his head sadly and stupidly.

"Don't you pretend." And the soldiers fell on him, punching, kicking. "Lead the way at once! Get going!" they bawled out. Helpless, he turned to lead them to Karabash. Soaking wet, and with the butt of a gun held to his back, he walked and walked and — walked. If he stopped to get the mud out of

his soggy shoes, the gun pushed him forward. "Wise Fatima," the Hodja thought, "who had said *insha' Allah*." Towards sunset the Hodja staggered into Karabash.

Having no money in his pocket, or friends in Karabash to spend the night there, the Hodja started back home. Still raining, it soon turned dark. Slipping and falling, the Hodja thought again of the wise Fatima, who always said *insha' Allah*, asleep in her warm bed.

It was midnight when Nasiruddin Hodja reached home. He gave a thankful sigh when he leaned on his door, and banged to awaken the sleeping Fatima.

"Who is there?" she called from inside.

"Oh, Fatima," the Hodja answered, in a rather soft and low voice. "It...is...I.., *Insha' Allah*."

Soup of the Soup

O ne day there was a loud knock on the street door of the Hodja's house. "Who can that be?" he wondered, as he hurried across the courtyard. When he opened the door, there stood Hussein from the village. He held out a nice fat rabbit in his hand. He grinned and said: "I shot that just for you, Hodja Effendi."

"How good of you, Hussein! And what a plump rabbit!" The Hodja's mouth watered as he thought of the tasty dish the rabbit would make. "Fatima," he called, "come and see what our friend Hussein has brought us from the village."

Fatima pulled her veil over her face, and joined her husband. As she took the rabbit from his hand, the Hodja said to Hussein, "Stay and eat with us; my Fatima is a good cook." To Fatima he said: "Make your nicest meal, Fatima."

Nasiruddin Hodja was most happy as he thought of the lunch ahead of him. He was also happy to have someone to listen to him. The two men sat cross-legged on the floor. The Hodja talked, and Hussein listened.

At last, after about two hours, the strong odour of rabbit floated in. Soon the door opened and Fatima entered with steaming rich pilav and rabbit, and thin rounds of roti to go with it. The men began to eat.

"What good cooking!" Hussein exclaimed. "The ginger and garlic and spices are just right. Your wife is a great cook."

"And what rabbit! The fat dripping to give taste to the rice!" With pieces of the roti they wiped their plates clean. Their stomachs now bulged round under their cloaks, and their waistbands got too tight. "We still have the rabbit bones," the Hodja said. "Fatima makes excellent soups. She will work on that next."

Thanking the Hodja, Hussein the villager said goodbye and left. When he reached the village, he told all his friends about the goodness of the hodja, and what a good cook his wife was.

The next morning, again the Hodja heard a knock on his door. Standing outside were two strangers. The Hodja looked at their hands. They hung empty by their sides. "Who may you be wanting to see?" he asked.

"Uh ..." the men smiled shyly. "We are the neighbours of Hussein who brought you the rabbit yesterday." And they looked as if they would like to be invited in.

"Come in, come in," the Hodja said. "Hussein is such a nice man. His neighbours are certainly very welcome."

"Hussein spoke so well of you; he said you treated him like a king," they said. And they seemed to sniff the air, which was full of the odour of Fatima's soup today.

"Stay and eat with me," said the Hodja, feeling like a king. "Fatima," he called, "our visitors will stay for lunch." To the visitors he said, "My wife is making soup with the bones of the rabbit."

Before long, Fatima brought in three steaming bowls smelling good and rich.

The men ate, and the Hodja talked. But he did not talk half as much as the day before. The meal over, the villagers thanked the Hodja, and left to tell of his kindness. The next morning, a knock was heard once again. Two more men stood there. The Hodja looked at their empty hands.

"What can I do for you?" he asked softly.

"Uh ..." they grinned. "We are the neighbours of the neighbours of Hussein who brought you the rabbit. They spoke so much of your kindness."

These villagers also looked as if they would like to come in. "Come in and share what we have," the Hodja offered kindly.

The men came in and sat down and waited. The Hodja went into the kitchen. In the same bowl was just one spoonful left of yesterday's rabbit bone soup. The Hodja poured a kettle of hot water over this, stirred it, poured it into three bowls and brought them out.

"O neighbours of the neighbours of Hussein who brought me the rabbit," he said aloud, "please enjoy the soup of the soup of the bones of the rabbit."

One neighbour of the neighbours of Hussein picked up his bowl. Two grains of rice and a piece of carrot floated in his hot water. The other neighbour of the neighbours of Hussein picked up his bowl. In the hot water floated two grains of rice and a piece of onion.

Nasiruddin Hodja made a big show of eating his soup with great relish. Then he led his guests to the door with many smiles. And the next day, the Hodja and his wife sat down to a quiet meal by themselves once more.

The Honoured Guests

Nasiruddin Hodja had been working in his vineyard. His vines had to be cut and tied, and tidied up. This had taken all day. For once, he thought, he had really worked very hard. A wash, my supper, and I will deserve my bed, he thought, as he rode back home on his faithful donkey.

As the donkey plodded into Ak Shehir, he noticed people in posh clothes going somewhere. Now where could they be going? He wondered. "Hodja Effendi, are you not coming?" someone asked.

"Of course I'm coming," the Hodja answered, pretending not to be ignored. "Is it today?"

"Certainly it is today; and Halil Effendi always entertains well. Hurry, or you will be late."

"Don't worry, I'll be there," the Hodja called back. So the dinner was at Halil Effendi's. Had he been invited? Why, of course, he could not be left out. Anyway, he was going.

"Oh Hodja Effendi, hurry! Hurry, or you won't make it," called another passerby.

The sun was low in the western sky. "But if I go home first," the Hodja said to himself, "and wash and change into fresh clothes, I will certainly be late for the dinner." So he made the donkey turn in the opposite direction to go straight to Halil's house.

At Halil's, the guests had all arrived. They were gathered inside, and chatting with one another. The Hodja tied his donkey in the courtyard, left his shoes at the door, and walked in. There was a broad smile on his face, and he was ready with all his jokes. Soon he was tapping his friends on the shoulder, and telling his yarns, but he discovered that no one was listening to him. He was talking to the backs of the people.

Halil himself was receiving the guests and showing them to their places.

"Salaam Aleykum, Halil Effendi," the Hodja said, going forward to greet him. But Halil had turned and was greeting someone else! "I think I know," said the Hodja to himself. He went out, got on his donkey, and went straight home.

"Fatima," he called, as he entered the courtyard from the street. "Get me water for a wash. And soap. Put out my best coat and my new turban. And brush my new shoes. I'm going to Halil's house for dinner. I'm already late."

Fatima rushed around. She poured fresh cold water into the stone basin in the yard, and placed a jug beside it. She brought the soap and the towel. Then she ran inside for the fresh clothes. She also took out his pair of good shoes, spat on them, and brushed them with a thick cloth.

The Hodja was soon dressed in his best clothes, and was looking almost like a bridegroom! Fatima looked proudly at him. She had not seen him so well dressed in years. Then he picked up his stick and set off for Halil's house.

He walked down the lanes with great dignity. Even the little boys who passed him, stopped to greet him. The women looked at him coyly from behind their windows, admiring him. "Come see," they called the others, "see the Hodja today!"

So Nasiruddin Hodja reached Halil's house. This time, as he entered the courtyard, Halil came out. He flung out both arms to welcome him. "Do come in, my good friend," he said, "we are all waiting for you." Halil led him to one low table and seated him there with a group.

The steaming food was brought in and laid on the tables,

and the guests began to dip their fingers in the dishes, and help themselves. Suddenly, those near the Hodja stopped eating, to watch him.

The Hodja picked up some pilav and fed it to his coat. 'Eat, my coat, eat," he said. Next he placed a piece of meat in his pocket. "That's for you," he said.

"WHAT! What are you doing?" asked the surprised guests around him.

"And why do you do that?" asked Halil.

"When I came earlier," answered the Hodja, "you did not know me, and turned your backs on me. But now thát I am in my best clothes and shoes, I am your honoured guest. I think it is my clothes you are honouring...and not me. I am therefore feeding your honoured guests!"

The Learned Men

One day a letter came for Nasiruddin Hodja Effendi. "For me!" exclaimed the Hodja, greatly surprised. "A letter!"

"Yes," answered the messenger, "from the mayor."

The Hodja was even more surprised. Now, in those days, few letters were written, for not many knew how to read or to write. And the Hodja was one of those few learned men. He could slowly read out and spell the words; he could even write some of them.

The letter read:

"Three priests, very learned men, have come to our humble town. They wish to meet the learned men here, and ask questions of them. We plan a feast in their honour. You must come and meet them so that they can ask you their questions. You must come at once."

A feast and conversation! The Hodja liked nothing better; he was overjoyed. He did not stop to change his clothes or tidy up. He got on his donkey and was off.

Those were the days when learned men went to different towns meeting other learned men. They asked difficult questions of each other to prove who was the cleverer.

All the learned men of Ak Shehir were gathered at the Mayor's house. They warmly welcomed the Hodja and gladly pushed him to the front. There, before him sat and stood the distinguished visitors — men of great girth and height. They were dressed in fur-edged robes and rich turbans, and certainly looked down their noses at the Hodja! "So, this is the Hodja?" asked one coming forward, and looked him up and down — from the top of his untidy turban, down his bleached coat, his patched churidars, right down to the curl of his worn out shoes. How the Hodja wished he had washed, and changed into good clothes! However, the Hodja was ready for him. He drew himself up to his full height, and struck a learned pose, as he stood — one hand on his donkey, and one leg crossed over the other — and waited. "I will ask the first question," the learned man said, looking boldly at the Hodja.

"Where is the centre of the earth?"

At once the Hodja straightened up, and with the toe of his shabby shoe, pointed to the left hind foot of his donkey: "The centre of the earth," said he very knowingly, "is exactly under the left hind foot of my donkey."

"How can you be so sure of that?" asked the priest, staring hard at the left hind foot of the donkey.

"Oh, I just know," said the Hodja, very sure of himself. "Of course, if you do not believe me, you are free to measure it. If it is different, even by a finger's width, I will be the first to accept that you are the cleverer one."

The learned priest turned, scratching his chin, and signed to the next one to question him.

Now the second priest went up, glaring at the Hodja, "My question is: How — many stars — are there — in the sky?"

"There are as many stars in the sky," the Hodja answered slowly but very definitely, "as there are hairs on my donkey."

"How do you know that?" the visitor asked, upset.

"Oh, it is one of those things one just knows. Of course, if you can't accept it, you may count the stars in the sky and the hairs on my donkey, and make sure. If I am wrong — even by one extra star or hair — I'm willing to bow to you as the greater man."

The visitor looked stupidly at the donkey, and signed to the third man to take his turn.

The third priest was the most important. He looked down his nose and long beard, and barely noticing the Hodja, "Mine .. is only a simple question," he said. Then lifting his head high, he asked: "How many hairs — are there in my beard?" And he lovingly stroked his nice long beard.

"That has a very simple answer," said the Hodja, walking back to his donkey.

"There are as many hairs in your beard as there are hairs in my donkey's tail." He held up the tail.

The honourable priest was angry at this comparison. "How do you know that?" and he looked disdainfully at the donkey's broom of a tail.

"Why, it is one of the many things I just happen to know. And it will be simple enough to prove it," said the Hodja.

By now quite angry, the priest cried: "Yes, I do want you to prove it to me. I do not believe you at all."

That's fine," said the cool Hodja. "For every hair you pull off my donkey's tail, I will pull one off your chin. If there is but one hair more on my donkey's tail, or on your chin, it will prove me wrong and you right. And if you are proved right, you can go up and down the land proclaiming that you are more clever than the humble Hodja of Ak Shehir."

The learned priest covered his beard with his two hands, and quickly withdrew behind his brothers.

And the hungry Hodja wondered how soon the feast would begin.

Helping the Woodcutter

Nasiruddin Hodja was up on the mountains when he heard the voice of a man, the sound of someone cutting wood, and the tinkle of donkey bells.

A narrow path led up to a high spot. There he saw six donkeys contentedly grazing. On all sides were piles of wood neatly cut. On one side was a strong woodcutter quietly swinging his axe and cutting away at a tree. The Hodja stopped abruptly as a tall tree came down in front of him. Sitting on a stump in the cool shade was a cheerful young man, small, and neatly dressed. "Great!" he shouted when the tree came down. "Well done! That tree has a lot of wood in it, and it will keep Siraj-ed-Din Bey comfortably warm this winter. Now, on to the next tree."

The woodcutter seemed to take no notice of the little man, half his size. He went along, picked another tree, and began axing away. The chips flew this way and that. As the axe hit the wood, the little man would grunt as if he were swinging the axe! He whistled as the chips flew; groaned as the tree swayed and broke; and when it fell, he cheered! The Hodja grew curious.

"Why do you make all this noise?" he asked the little man, "when he is doing all the work?"

"Don't you see?" asked the little man. "I am helping the woodcutter in his work. He has agreed to cut thirty donkey-loads of wood for Siraj-ed-Din Bey. That's a lot of work for one man. I felt sorry for him and offered to be his partner. While he cuts, I give him courage and strength by cheering, grunting and groaning for him."

The Hodja listened to the little man. Then he looked at the muscular woodcutter, working away. "I think," he said, "it is not you who gives him strength and courage; it is his own strong arms and body." And turning his donkey he trotted away.

Two weeks later the Hodja was wandering near the court. Two men were quarrelling before the Judge. The Hodja recognised them. They were the same woodcutter and the little man.

"I earned every ghurush of it myself," the woodcutter was saying. "I cut the thirty loads of wood. I loaded them on to the donkeys, and drove them to the house of Siraj-ed-Din Bey. There, I unloaded every single stick, and he rightly paid all the money to me as agreed upon."

"But he forgets," cried the other man, "how I grunted and groaned, clapped and cheered him as he worked. Without my companionship and support, would he have been able to do all that work? Surely I earned half the pay for what I did? And the Bey gives him all the money. Half of it must come to me."

The Judge looked confused and helpless. Never in his life had he heard a case like this! Suddenly his eyes fell on the Hodja, elbowing his way through the crowd. "Hodja Effendi!" he was glad to welcome him. "Have you ever heard of a problem like this?"

"Now tell him, one at a time," he said to the quarrelling men.

The woodcutter and the little man told their stories till there was nothing more to tell.

The Hodja called a court attendant. "Bring me a tray," he said. Turning to the woodcutter, he said: "Hand me your bag of money." "But it is all mine," cried the frightened man. "With my hard work and sweat I earned every ghurush of it!"

"Give it to me," said the Hodja. Very unwillingly the woodcutter handed it over.

The little man, with a big greedy smile, came closer to the tray. His eyes were glued to it.

The Hodja took the tray and the money. He took a coin from the bag and rang it out on the tray. "You see that ghurush?" he asked the little man. "It's a good coin, isn't it? And do you like the sound of it?"

"Yes, yes," the little man said expectantly.

The Hodja took out another coin and rang it. "Do you hear that? Doesn't it sound good?"

The little man drew so close that his nose almost touched the tray. And his fingers itched for the feel of the silver coins.

The woodcutter meanwhile was anxious and miserable. Would he lose some of his hard-earned money? Money that was only his? And so, the Hodja rang out every coin in the money bag. "You heard all the coins, didn't you?" he asked of the little man. The little man nodded hopefully.

The Hodja then swept all the coins back into the bag.

"The sound of the money is sufficient pay for the sound of the work," he said to the little man.

And he handed the bag of money to the woodcutter, and said: "And this money is paid for the work itself."

Allah's Gift of Money

One day the Hodja was acting rather strangely. He spread his prayer rug in his courtyard. He then knelt on it, sat back straight, and bent his head, praying loudly. "Oh Allah," he cried, "I want money very urgently. I want one thousand ghurush. Not one less or more — just one thousand. Please send me this — and quickly."

Whether Allah heard it or not, all his neighbours heard it. His close neighbour, Siraj-ed-Din Bey, the richest man in Ak Shehir — he heard it too and smiled to himself.

"Oh Allah, if you send me nine hundred or nine hundred and ninety nine, I will not accept it; only one thousand ghurush," the Bey heard him say.

"I'll play a joke on him," Siraj-ed-din Bey said to his wife. He went into his little room and counted out nine hundred and ninety nine ghurush. He counted a second time to make sure it was only one less than a thousand. Then he put it into a cloth bag, and tied it tight. As the Hodja prayed, he flung it from his window, into the Hodja's yard. The bag clinked down near the Hodja — just a little away from his bald head.

Quickly the Hodja snatched up the bag. He sat up and counted the money — once, twice. Nine hundred and ninety nine — whichever way he counted!

They Bey and his wife were watching the Hodja, unseen form behind their window. They laughed as the Hodja kept counting. Did he not pray that he would not accept anything less than a thousand?

The Hodja went down on his knees. He put his forehead to the ground. "Allah, thank you for sending me the money, but you counted wrong! You sent me one ghurush less. Please send that as soon as it is convenient." Then he put the money back in the bag, and tucked it safely away in his waistband.

At this the Bey shot out of his house. He rushed to the Hodja's street door and banged on it. The neighbours, seeing the wealthy Bey so furiously banging on the Hodja's door, gathered round.

"Give me back my money," yelled the Bey.

"Your money?" asked the Hodja, surprised.

"Yes. I threw that bag of money with nine hundred and ninety nine ghurush in it, from my window. I heard you pray to Allah, and say that you will not take anything less than a thousand ghurush. I did it as a joke."

"You threw it? No, Allah gave it to me in answer to my prayer. Straight from heaven it dropped," the Hodja said.

"I will take you to court," the Bey yelled.

"Yes, let the honourable Judge decide," agreed the Hodja.

"Come on then. Right away," the Bey ordered.

"Oh," said the Hodja, "How can I go to court without a coat? My wife is mending mine."

"I will lend you a coat. You can wear mine," the Bey offered.

"And my donkey is lame today," cried the Hodja.

"Well," said the Bey, "you can ride on my horse."

"But my donkey's saddle will not fit your horse."

"Come to my house," the Bey yelled, not wishing to waste any more time. "I will fit you out with a bridle and saddle."

The Hodja waved his hand in the direction of his window. Fatima was sure to be watching behind it.

In the Bey's house, the Hodja put on the Bey's rich coat;

climbed on to his fine horse, and sat astride on the embroidered saddle and set off.

In the court, Siraj-ed-Din Bey promptly told the Judge his story. Then he looked at the Hodja. The Hodja was looking at the Bey with much sadness on his face, and sighing and shaking and shaking his head.

"Well, Nasiruddin Hodja, have you anything to say?" asked the Judge.

"Poor Siraj-ed-Din Bey! My honoured friend and neighbour. It is so very very sad," answered the Hodja, "that he is out of his mind."

"Out of his mind! What do you mean?" asked the Judge.

"Didn't you know?" And the Hodja whispered to the Judge, loud enough for everyone to hear. "What is more, he thinks he owns everything. He told you about my money bag. Now ask him if he owns my coat.

"Of course, that is my coat," cried the Bey, even before being asked. "The Hodja knows full well that it is mine."

"He will say now that the saddle on my horse too is his," continued the Hodja.

"Yes, the saddle and the bridle too," said the Bey.

"What's left? You will own my horse too," went on the Hodja.

"Honourable Judge, that horse has been mine since it was a colt."

The Judge had had enough proof now.

"Dear Bey," he said sadly, "I think you have been working too hard. You should go home and take a long rest. I almost believed you about the money Bey, though it was a strange joke throwing so much money out like that."

To the Hodja he said: "Nasiruddin, you may keep your money bag, and your coat, your horse and everything."

Poor Siraj-ed-Din Bey was in a confused state of mind. And he looked very sad and old as he turned home. But the Hodja came bouncing behind. The two men rode in silence. When the Bey turned in at his gate, he found the Hodja following him in.

"Here is your money bag," he said to the surprised Bey, "and your coat and your bridle, saddle and horse."

As the Bey watched, speechless, the Hodja said: "Wasn't it fun to confuse that learned old Judge? I am now going to him, to tell him that it was all a joke!"

"Ride my horse," offered the Bey.

"Oh, no! My donkey ought to be all right now, and Fatima will have mended my coat."

The One-Legged Goose

Nasiruddin Hodja was on his way to Tamerlane's palace. Under his left arm, he held tightly, a roasted goose. The clever Fatima had specially roasted a goose as a gift for their royal friend. The Hodja took large strides as he walked, the sooner to reach the palace. With his right hand he held his nose tight, so that the tempting aroma of the roasted goose might not make him nibble of a piece.

A fly suddenly flew into his eyes. The Hodja's right hand shot at for a second. But that was long enough for the delicious smell of the roast goose to race through his nose to his brain. The roast goose must really taste nice since Fatima cooked it, he thought. When was it, he wondered, that he had last tasted roast goose? It seemed so very long ago. And his stomach was empty and hungry.

The great Tamerlane may not mind the Hodja tasting a tiny piece — like one juicy leg, maybe? He may not even miss it. After all Tamerlane must be eating roast goose every day. And, so the Hodja was soon biting away at the leg he had pulled off.

Would the Emperor notice the missing leg, he wondered? What explanation would he give? The answer would come to him when the Emperor asked the question, he told himself; and quickly finished the last bits of meat off the bone.

Soon he was at the palace. Tamerlane was alone and glad to see the Hodja. He was even more glad to see the Hodja's gift.

"A goose! And roasted by Fatima! It will be GOOD!" he exclaimed as if he had never eaten goose before.

The Hodja talked away as the greatly pleased emperor turned the gift over and over, praising it.

"Yes, your Majesty, Fatima is a fine cook." He talked about Fatima's pilavs, her soups, her stews, her sweets — but the Emperor interrouted him.

"Strange! How strange! This goose has only one leg?"

The Hodja was looking out of the window, and looking for inspiration too.

"One leg? What did you expect, your Majesty?"

"Why, two of course!" retorted Tamerlane.

"Two legs! Not here, your Majesty! Geese in other towns may have two, or even four legs; but the geese of Ak Shehir are famous for being one-legged."

"That is a tall story!" Tamerlane replied, quite angry, guessing what had happened. "You know very well what happened to the other leg."

"Judge for yourself," called the Hodja, from the window. "Look at those geese in your own yard."

Tamerlane came to the window. There stood the geese asleep in the midday heat.

"I count twelve geese, and I count twelve legs. Do they count differently here, your Majesty?" the Hodja asked.

The Emperor counted. "One…nine …eleven, twelve." Sure enough each goose had only one leg! The Emperor was confused. "I'm…sure…that in the town where I grew up… I thought the geese had two legs each."

"Yes, your Majesty," the Hodja said kindly, "that does happen in certain places. But in Ak Shehir, they have always been one-legged. Now I must be going," he said in a great hurry. "*Salaam Aleykum,*" he called, with a deep bow, and his hand to his forehead, as he left.

"*Ve Aleykum*! But funny!" said the Emperor to himself. "And I never noticed this all these years. I've been so busy fighting wars, and ruling the land; I've not noticed the geese..."

At that moment, a camel which was also asleep in the yard suddenly stretched and squealed. And his voice was loud and shrill as he screamed. At once the geese came awake. Out plopped their other legs, tucked under their wings, as they stretched and hissed, and scattered in all directions.

It was just at this moment that the Hodja came under the window where Tamerlane stood. Coming to his senses, the Emperor stuck his head out. What he yelled at the Hodja sounded more like the cry of a wounded animal, and not the dignified words of an Emperor to a subject, who had just brought him a gift.

Before the Hodja left the yard, he called out: "But, my Emperor, if you or I heard such a noise while asleep, we too would sprout at least four legs!"

And Tamerlane smiled inspite of himself.

He turned to his roasted goose, pulled off the remaining leg, and bit into its juicy meat.

"What a lovely roast! What a fine cook!" he exclaimed.

The Mixed-up Feet

The village boys were all the Hodja's friends, and they loved to play jokes on him. But most times the Hodja played it back on the boys, and the joke would be on them.

One day four boys were playing in a small stream. They saw the Hodja coming along. He was sitting on his donkey, his feet almost touching the ground. The donkey trotted along with the Hodja half asleep on its back.

"Let's play a trick on the Hodja," said Ali.

"Yes, yes," Muhammad agreed.

"What trick shall we play?" asked Hassan.

"Think fast," said the fourth boy.

The boys put their heads close together, and began to plot. One pointed to their feet, and whispered something. "For sure!" they all agreed. The boys stood still as if their feet had taken root in the stream.

Soon the sleepy Hodja trotted up alongside the boys. He saw the boys huddled together in the stream. So still and looking down! "What could they be doing?" he wondered. He stopped his donkey; he had to find out.

The boys held each other tight. They planted their feet even more firmly and stared down into the water.

The Hodja got off his donkey and went towards the boys. "Hullo, boys!" he called out. "What are you looking at?"

"Oh, Hodja Sir," cried Ali, "please help us. We are in great trouble."

"Please help us" said Hassan, "or we will have to stay here for the rest of our lives!"

"What is the matter" cried the Hodja, now close to them.

"It's our feet!" cried Ahmed. "They are all mixed up. Muhammad says the big feet are his, but I think they are mine."

"The foot with the cut on is mine," said Ali, "but Hassan says he too has a cut on his foot. I can easily tell that is my foot."

And so the boys went on, while they stared at their feet in the water.

The Hodja walked back to the donkey. He pulled off its back a thick stick that he always carried. And as he neared the boys, he said "I'll help you find your legs." And he threw the stick at them.

Quick as lightning the boys found their feet. They rushed out of the water and were on the bank, before the stick could reach them.

"Glad I could be of help to you, boys," the Hodja said with a grin. "Next time you are in trouble, be sure to let me know."

The boys laughed sheepishly.

"This Hodja is just too clever for us," the boys said to themselves. "We can't play tricks on him."

A Gift for the King

One day the Hodja was working in his garden. There, on his plum tree the plums were ripening. The Hodja was sure that his trees had the sweetest plums in all the world.

"I will pluck the best and take them to the king as a gift," he said. He picked three lovely plums. He put them on a copper tray, balanced it on his head, and off he marched to the king's palace.

As the Hodja walked along, the plums rolled from side to side on his tray. "There are too many on this tray," the Hodja said to himself, "so they keep quarrelling with each other. I must punish them. I will eat one of them. Then the remaining two will sit quietly, behaving themselves."

He took out one of the plums and ate it. "Mmm!" he said, as its sweetness flowed into his mouth. "I knew mine are the sweetest plums! It's a pity only two are left for the king! But...he must be eating sweet plums all the time."

But the plums were still rolling on his tray. The Hodja got angry, and ate one more to keep the other in place. Now there was only one plum left on the tray. And it stayed in place till he got to the king.

At the palace, Tamerlane was in a happy mood that day. "What a nice man — the Hodja — to think of bringing me a gift! Even if it is only one plum off his tree. Fill his tray with gifts," he ordered. And the Hodja returned home loaded with the king's gifts.

Some time later, the Hodja thought it was time to take another gift to the king. He took some of the best beetroots in his garden, heaped them on the tray, and set off.

On the way to the palace, he met his friend Ali. "Are you taking beetroot for the king? Nobody gives beetroot as a gift, least of all, to the king." Ali told him.

"Then what shall I give him?" asked the Hodja.

"Well, maybe you can take him some juicy figs, fresh from the trees."

"That's a good idea," said the Hodja, pleased with the advice. "I'll go on to the market-place. There I will trade these good beetroots for figs." The Hodja set off for the market.

In the market, the Hodja found a man selling figs.

"These are just ready to eat," he said. "They will melt in your mouth."

The Hodja traded his fresh beetroot for a lot of figs. But the fig-seller was a real crook. He took the Hodja's good beetroots, and gave him a lot of overripe soft figs which would go bad the next day.

But he had placed the figs neatly on the Hodja's tray. The Hodja picked up his tray, placed it on his head, and set off to the palace.

At the palace, the king was in one of his terrible moods. It was then that the Hodja arrived with the tray full of over-ripe figs ready to burst. That made him more angry.

"Come here at once," he called to his servants. The servants came running. "Throw these figs at the Hodja; every one of them," he ordered. "And don't you miss a single throw."

The servants began aiming at the Hodja. He turned and ran.

But the figs followed him. As they struck him, the over-ripe figs burst like tomatoes all over him. The Hodja raced home, with fig juice sprayed all over.

Meeting Ali, a few days later, the Hodja said: "I must thank you, brother, for your very good advice."

"What was that?" asked Ali.

"You told me not to take beetroots as a gift to any one, least of all to a king. What if they had pelted me with the hard beets instead of the soft figs? I would have been black and blue all over. Allah be praised for my escape!"

Buying a New Donkey

Donkeys all over the world are known for being stubborn, and the Hodja's donkey was no different from any other donkey. It would sometimes make up its little mind not to go any further. Then it would stand still and not budge an inch. No matter how much the Hodja coaxed it or hit it, or tweaked its tail, the donkey would not move.

"I will not keep this donkey even for one more day," the angry Hodja shouted to his wife one day.

"Maybe the new one will be even worse," his wife, Fatima, suggested. "Nothing can be worse than this one," the Hodja said. "No other donkey, I am sure, could eat more and be as slow, as stubborn, and as stupid. I will take him to the market this very day and sell him and get some money instead, with that I will buy another donkey, and I hope I will have some money left over too."

So the Hodja got on his donkey and set off for the market-place, riding his donkey for the last time.

At the animal market there were a lot of animals. There were many buyers also, standing around, inspecting the donkeys for sale. One man stood on a high stone. He was selling the animals. People bid for the animals. That is, one man called out a price, and if another wanted the same animal and was willing to pay a higher price for it, he shouted out his higher price or bid, and so on. The one who called out the highest price got the animal. This kind of buying is called an auction, and this is how people there bought or sold their animals.

The Hodja rode up and tied his donkey for inspection. Loudly, he said to the man who was selling: "Here is a fine donkey I want you to sell for me." All those standing around could hear him. "I would never give this donkey away: but I need the money, so I am selling it."

The auctioneer or the man who was selling the animals, looked at the Hodja's donkey. "Yes," he agreed, "It is a fine animal." The Hodja went all round looking at the other donkeys standing there. He then chose one of those to buy when its turn came.

One by one, the seller put up the animals for sale. The men bid for them, and all the donkeys were sold, except two. One was the Hodja's and the other, the one he had chosen to buy. The seller then brought up to the front, the Hodja's donkey. "Such a fine animal you will never see!" he exclaimed. "Look at him...he looks wise...and obedient."

The Hodja looked at his donkey as if he had never seen it before. He did seem to have a wise look about him. The donkey also stood and waited there obediently and patiently. "This donkey must be a very patient and obedient donkey," he said to himself.

The seller went on: "His master has taken good care of him. His legs are strong, and he looks such a healthy animal." The Hodja looked closely at him once again.

"Just think of the loads he can carry," the seller coaxed. By now the Hodja was sure this was the best of animals. Then the bidding started.

"Fifty ghurush." A voice called out. This was a very low bid. The Hodja was furious. "My fine animal for only fifty ghurush! Two liras!" he called. (One hundred ghurush would make one lira.) A villager bid above that, and up and up went the price. Every so often the Hodja would raise the bid: "Four ...six ...ten liras."

Finally one man called "ten liras and five ghurush!"

The Hodja put his hand into the pocket of his baggy trousers, pulled out his cloth purse, and counted all the money he had. "Ten liras and eleven ghurush!" he called.

After that no one bid anymore. The Hodja counted out all his money to the auctioneer, got on the back of the fine donkey, and rode home.

Suddenly he thought, on his way home, "How is it that I don't have any money in my pocket?"

Can you tell him why?

The Bear in the Pear Tree

The mountainside was lonely except for the Hodja, who was cutting wood today. The ring of his axe could be heard, as it echoed through the forest. Soon the Hodja sat down to rest.

There was a great silence as he rested. Only the twitter and singing of birds could be heard; or the hum and buzz of insects; or the rustle of leaves and twigs as they fell from the trees.

Suddenly, something made the Hodja nearly jump out of his skin! Crackle...crunch...crunch! It came steadily to him through the forest floor. What could that be? It was not the sound of a squirrel, or rabbit or fox. The Hodja was still and listened carefully, as he stared in the direction of the sound.

Crackle ..crunch...crunch! It came steadily nearer, and grew louder and louder. Then... he saw black fur and four black stiff legs coming straight towards him! It also had a shiny nose between two sharp eyes. It was the biggest bear the Hodja had seen in all his life!

The Hodja did not stop to think or make sure. He shot out for the nearest tree. It was a wild pear tree. He climbed up that tree faster than he had ever done in his boyhood days.

Crackle...crunch...crunch! Was that bear coming straight to the pear tree? Yes.. it was! It stopped right at the foot of the pear tree where the Hodja was hiding! It yawned widely, and then...it lay down to sleep!

The Hodja climbed up higher and hid among the branches there. "You won't fool me that way, old bear," he murmured. "You'll pretend you're asleep, and then you will pounce on me when I come down. I'll stay right here."

The big black bear went to sleep, and was soon snoring loudly below. The Hodja sat in his uncomfortable perch and waited. From the mosque across the valley came the mullah's call to prayer: "*Allah-ho-Akbar!*"

"That means it is two hours to sunset," the Hodja told himself. But the big black bear still snored loudly below. Perched on the branch, in the same position all the time, the Hodja felt pins and needles pricking him all over. He slowly shifted to a more comfortable position. A shower of twigs and leaves fell on the heavily sleeping bear below. The sun went further down in the sky. The call to prayer floated over the trees to him a second time.

"That is sunset now," said the Hodja to himself. He shifted his stiff body a little. But the bear — he slept peacefully down below.

Once more the voices of the mullahs came floating up to him. "That's two hours after sunset," he said. He turned in the direction of Mecca, and prayed to Allah for help. Soon it was bright moonlight. The Hodja, still stiff and cramped on top, could dimly see the black body stretched out down below.

At last, the bear awoke. He shivered, and stretched. He then stood up on his four stiff legs, and sniffed hungrily. The next moment ...he dug his claws into the trunk of the tree, and up he climbed!

The poor Hodja trembled so much that he was almost falling off. The bear sniffed and searched till he found what he wanted...a nice juicy wild pear. His paws went all over looking for more. Eating and climbing, the bear went up and up. Shivering and quaking, the Hodja climbed higher and higher. He soon reached the highest branch that could bear his weight. "Oh Allah," he prayed, "please keep the bear satisfied below."

Smack! Smack! went the bear's lips over the juicy pears. The bear seemed so close...the Hodja was trembling all over. Soon its breath was almost on the Hodja's face behind the leaves. Suddenly, one paw swung out at a pear, almost into the mouth of the Hodja, as if the bear wanted to share it with him.

At this, the trembling Hodja yelled: "No, Thank you. I don't care for pears... I never eat them...."

Now the bear was really a shy old bear, afraid of the world around him. He had never heard a strange voice like this yell at him though the leaves high up on a tree!

The bear was so shocked, he just let go of the branch. He came crashing through the branches, and landed in a heap at the foot of the tree. And there he lay ....still, never to move again.

The Hodja spent the rest of the night on the tree, and then came down slowly....a little at a time. By early morning he was on the lowest branch. As the sun's rays fell on the bear, the Hodja could see that big black bear would not frighten anyone any more. It was dead and stiff.

The Hodja came down, picked up his axe, and set off, limping his way home. "But what a story I will have to tell everybody!" he thought to himself. Then, he had a better idea. His usual grin spread across his face. He pulled out his knife, ran back to the bear and skinned it.

The Hodja threw the bear's skin over his shoulders, and marched off to Ak Shehir. He came down the mountainside, singing loudly in his cracked voice. When he neared the town, he avoided the shortest route home. He walked through the main road, by the marketplace, and through one busy street after another. He did not need to open his mouth.

Word spread about the brave and wonderful Hodja, who had killed the biggest black bear!

A-RUP/6463/3/3